Stress Management in the Workplace

Strategies for a Healthier Work Life

By

Dr Martina Jonesson

Table of Contents

3. <u>Resilience Training for Employees</u>
4. <u>Diversity, Inclusion, and Stress Management</u>

Conclusion

Introduction

In the pursuit of professional success and meeting the demands of the modern workplace, employees often find themselves caught up in the whirlwind of work-related responsibilities, deadlines, and pressures. While dedicating time and effort to excel in their careers is essential, it is equally vital for individuals to prioritize their well-being outside of work. Nurturing self-care beyond the office walls is a fundamental aspect of managing workplace stress effectively and fostering a healthier, more balanced life.

In the preceding chapters, we explored an array of stress management techniques, from creating a supportive work environment to coping with difficult situations and implementing stress-relief exercises at work. While these strategies undoubtedly contribute to enhancing the work experience, the journey towards stress reduction does not end when the workday concludes. It is during personal time that individuals have the opportunity to truly invest in their mental, emotional, and physical health.

In this chapter, we will delve into the significance of nurturing self-care outside of work as an integral part of a comprehensive stress management approach. We will explore various self-care practices that empower individuals to restore balance, recharge their energy, and build resilience for the challenges that await them in the workplace.

By nurturing self-care beyond work hours, employees cultivate a harmonious integration of their personal and professional lives. Restful sleep, engaging in physical activities, spending quality time with loved ones, pursuing hobbies, and practicing mindfulness are just a few examples of self-care practices that contribute to overall well-being.

Organizations that prioritize and encourage self-care recognize the value of their employees' holistic health. A culture that promotes self-care fosters an environment where employees feel supported, valued, and empowered to prioritize their well-being. As a result, employees are better equipped to handle workplace stress with clarity, focus, and emotional equilibrium.

Let us embark on a journey of self-discovery, exploring the transformative power of self-care in enhancing our resilience, improving our mental health, and ultimately creating a more balanced and fulfilling life. By embracing self-care practices, both within and outside the workplace, individuals can unlock their full potential, leading to a happier, healthier, and more successful professional journey. In the upcoming sections, we will explore specific self-care practices and their profound impact on stress management and overall well-being.

Chapter 1

Understanding Workplace Stress

Introduction to Workplace Stress:
Workplace stress is a prevalent issue affecting employees in various industries and job roles. The modern work environment often demands high performance, productivity, and adaptability, which can lead to significant stress levels among employees. In this chapter, we will delve into the definition and causes of workplace stress, explore common stressors in different work environments, and discuss the profound impact of stress on an individual's well-being and job performance.

1. Definition of Workplace Stress

Workplace stress refers to the physical, emotional, and psychological strain experienced by individuals due to pressures and demands in their work environment. It arises from a combination of factors such as excessive workload, tight deadlines, inadequate resources, organisational changes, lack of job control, and interpersonal conflicts. Understanding the root causes of workplace stress is crucial to implementing effective stress management strategies.

2. Common Stressors in Different Work Environments

Different work environments may present unique stressors that employees face daily. For example:
- Corporate Settings: High-pressure corporate jobs often involve tight project deadlines, performance evaluations, and competition among colleagues.
- Healthcare Professions: Healthcare workers experience stress from long working hours, emotionally demanding patient interactions, and the need to make critical decisions quickly.
- Educational Settings: Teachers and educators may encounter stress due to heavy workloads, administrative demands, and the responsibility of shaping young minds.
- Service Industry: Employees in customer-facing roles may experience stress from dealing with difficult customers and managing time-sensitive tasks.

3. The Impact of Workplace Stress on Physical and Mental Health

Workplace stress can have severe consequences on an individual's health. Prolonged exposure to stress hormones like cortisol can lead to:
- Increased risk of cardiovascular diseases, hypertension, and immune system suppression.
- Mental health issues include sadness, anxiety, and burnout.
- Sleep disturbances and disruptions in appetite and digestion.
- Decreased cognitive function, memory issues, and attention problems.

4. The Connection between Stress and Job Performance

Stress not only affects an individual's health but also significantly impacts their job performance and overall productivity. Some of the ways in which workplace stress influences job performance include:
- Reduced concentration and focus, leading to mistakes and decreased efficiency.

- Decreased job satisfaction and engagement, resulting in lower motivation and commitment to tasks.
- Increased absenteeism and presenteeism (being physically present but not fully functioning) due to stress-related health issues.
- Higher turnover rates as workers look for healthier workplaces.

5. Identifying Signs and Symptoms of Workplace Stress

It's essential for both employees and employers to recognize the signs of workplace stress early on to address the issue promptly. Common signs and symptoms of workplace stress include:
- Fatigue and low energy levels, even after sufficient rest.
- Anger, mood swings, or overwhelming feelings.
- Physical symptoms like headaches, tight muscles, and stomach problems.
- Withdrawal from social relations and a decline in interest in extracurricular activities.
- Decreased performance, missing deadlines, or increased errors.

In Summary

Understanding workplace stress is the first step toward implementing effective stress management strategies. By recognizing the causes and impact of stress, individuals and organisations can work together to create a healthier work environment that supports the well-being and productivity of employees. In the following chapters, we will explore various techniques and approaches to managing workplace stress and promoting a more balanced work life.

Chapter 2

The Impact of Stress on Health and Performance

Introduction:

In Chapter 1, we discussed the definition and common stressors in the workplace. Now, we will explore the profound impact of workplace stress on an individual's health and job performance. Understanding how stress affects both physical and mental well-being is crucial to recognizing its detrimental effects and taking proactive measures to manage and reduce it effectively.

1. Chronic Stress and Health Issues

Chronic workplace stress can take a toll on an individual's physical health, leading to various medical conditions. Some of the health issues associated with prolonged exposure to stress include:

- Cardiovascular Problems: Chronic stress is linked to an increased risk of hypertension, heart disease, and strokes. Stress hormones can elevate blood pressure and strain the cardiovascular system.
- Immune System Suppression: Prolonged stress can suppress the immune system, making individuals more susceptible to infections and illnesses.
- Digestive Disorders: Stress can disrupt digestive processes, leading to issues such as irritable bowel syndrome (IBS) and acid reflux.
- Musculoskeletal Conditions: Tension and muscle tightness caused by stress can result in headaches, back pain, and other musculoskeletal problems.

2. Stress and Mental Health

The impact of workplace stress on mental health is equally significant. Prolonged stress can contribute to the development or exacerbation of mental health disorders, including:
- Anxiety Disorders: Chronic stress can trigger or intensify symptoms of anxiety, leading to excessive worry, restlessness, and panic attacks.
- Depression: Feeling overwhelmed and stressed for an extended period may lead to feelings of sadness,

hopelessness, and a loss of interest in activities once enjoyed.

- Burnout: Burnout is a state of emotional, physical, and mental exhaustion caused by chronic workplace stress. It can result in a lack of motivation, reduced efficiency, and feelings of cynicism toward work.

3. Cognitive Function and Decision-making

Stress can impair cognitive function and decision-making abilities, negatively impacting job performance. When under stress, the brain's prefrontal cortex, responsible for rational thinking and decision-making, may become less effective. This can lead to:

- Reduced Concentration: Difficulty focusing on tasks and becoming easily distracted by stress-related thoughts.

- Memory Problems: Impaired short-term memory, which affects the ability to retain and recall information.

- Impulsive Behaviour: Stress may lead to impulsive decision-making rather than well-thought-out choices.

4. Workplace Productivity and Engagement

The effects of stress extend beyond an individual's health and can significantly impact workplace productivity and engagement. Some ways in which stress influences job performance include:

- Decreased Productivity: Stress can lead to reduced efficiency, as individuals may spend more time worrying or dealing with stress-related symptoms than focusing on their work tasks.

- Absenteeism and Presenteeism: Stressed employees may take more sick days or come to work while not fully functional, leading to a decline in overall productivity.

- Reduced Job Satisfaction: High levels of stress can contribute to job dissatisfaction, leading to decreased motivation and commitment to the organisation's goals.

In Summary

Recognizing the impact of workplace stress on health and performance is essential for both individuals and employers. Addressing stress-related issues proactively can lead to a healthier, more engaged workforce and improved overall productivity. In the following chapters, we will explore a variety of stress management techniques and strategies that can be implemented in the workplace to foster a positive and supportive work environment. By prioritising the well-being of employees and acknowledging the connection between stress and performance, organisations can create a thriving workplace culture that benefits everyone involved.

Chapter 3

Building a Resilient Mindset

Introduction:
In Chapter 2, we explored the profound impact of workplace stress on an individual's health and job performance. Building resilience is a powerful approach to effectively cope with workplace stress and its challenges. In this chapter, we will delve into the concept of resilience and provide strategies for cultivating a resilient mindset. A resilient mindset empowers individuals to navigate through stressful situations, adapt to changes, and maintain a healthier work-life balance.

1. Understanding Resilience

Resilience is the ability to bounce back from adversity, setbacks, and stressors. It involves a positive and adaptive response to challenges, enabling individuals to grow stronger and develop effective coping mechanisms. In the context of the workplace, resilience is essential for maintaining well-being and optimal performance, even in the face of high-pressure situations.

2. Techniques for Reframing Negative Thoughts

Negative thought patterns can intensify stress and hinder productivity. To build resilience, individuals can learn to reframe negative thoughts into more positive and constructive perspectives. Techniques for reframing negative thoughts include:

- Cognitive Restructuring: Identifying negative thought patterns and replacing them with more rational and realistic thoughts.
- Positive Affirmations: Practicing self-affirmations to boost self-esteem and counteract self-doubt.
- Gratitude Practice: Focusing on gratitude for positive aspects of work and life to shift the focus away from stressors.

3. Mindfulness and Stress Reduction

Mindfulness is a practice that involves being fully present and non-judgmentally aware of the current moment. It can help reduce stress by promoting relaxation and emotional regulation. Techniques for incorporating mindfulness into the workplace include:

- Mindful Breathing: Engaging in deep breathing exercises to calm the nervous system during stressful moments.

- Mindful Breaks: Taking short breaks throughout the workday to reset and refocus attention.

- Mindful Eating: Paying attention to the act of eating and savoring the flavors of food during meal times.

4. Developing a Growth Mindset

A growth mindset is the belief that abilities and intelligence can be developed through effort and learning. Embracing a growth mindset can enhance resilience by encouraging individuals to view challenges as opportunities for growth and learning. Ways to foster a growth mindset include:

- Embracing Challenges: Seeing challenges as stepping stones to improvement rather than obstacles to be avoided.

- Emphasizing Effort: Valuing effort and hard work over innate talent or intelligence.

- Learning from Failure: Viewing failures as opportunities to learn and improve rather than personal shortcomings.

5. Seeking Support and Building Social Connections

Social support is a crucial factor in building resilience. Having a strong support network at work can provide emotional assistance during stressful times and foster a sense of belonging. Strategies for seeking support and building social connections include:
- Connecting with Colleagues: Engaging in open and supportive communication with coworkers.
- Joining Work-related Groups: Participating in work-related clubs or organizations to build connections with like-minded individuals.
- Seeking Mentorship: Finding mentors or role models within the workplace to provide guidance and support.

In Summary

Cultivating a resilient mindset is essential for effectively managing workplace stress and enhancing overall well-being and performance. By reframing negative thoughts, practicing mindfulness, embracing a growth mindset, and fostering social connections, individuals can develop the resilience needed to thrive in challenging work environments. In the following chapters, we will explore additional stress management techniques that complement a resilient mindset, ultimately contributing to a healthier and happier work life.

Chapter 4

Effective Time and Task Management

Introduction:

In Chapter 3, we discussed building a resilient mindset to cope with workplace stress. Alongside resilience, effective time and task management are crucial skills for maintaining a healthier work-life balance. This chapter will focus on the significance of managing time and tasks efficiently to reduce stress, enhance productivity, and foster a more balanced work environment.

1. Time Management Strategies to Reduce Work-related Stress

Time management involves prioritizing tasks, allocating time effectively, and minimizing time-wasting activities. Implementing time management strategies can help reduce work-related stress by:

- Prioritizing Tasks: Identifying the most important and time-sensitive tasks to focus on first.
- Creating To-Do Lists: Organizing tasks in a list format to keep track of responsibilities and deadlines.
- Using Time Blocks: Allocating specific time blocks for different tasks to maintain focus and prevent multitasking.

2. Prioritization Techniques to Increase Productivity

Effectively prioritizing tasks enables individuals to allocate their time and energy to activities that have the most significant impact on their work and goals. Some prioritization techniques include:
- Eisenhower Matrix: Dividing tasks into four categories based on urgency and importance to determine the order of execution.
- ABC Analysis: Labeling tasks as A (urgent and important), B (important but not urgent), or C (not important and not urgent) to prioritize accordingly.
- Eat the Frog: Tackling the most challenging or unpleasant task first thing in the morning to gain momentum and motivation.

3. Setting Realistic Goals and Breaking Them Down into Manageable Tasks

Setting achievable and realistic goals is essential for reducing stress and maintaining motivation. Breaking larger goals into smaller, manageable tasks makes them less overwhelming and more attainable. This approach allows for steady progress without feeling overwhelmed by the enormity of the task.

4. Avoiding Multitasking and Focusing on Deep Work

Multitasking can lead to decreased productivity and increased stress. Encouraging individuals to focus on deep work, where they concentrate on one task at a time without distractions, can lead to more meaningful and efficient work outcomes.

5. Utilizing Technology and Tools for Time Management

There are various time management tools and apps available that can assist in organizing tasks, setting reminders, and tracking progress. Encouraging the use of such tools can help individuals manage their time effectively and reduce the risk of missing deadlines or forgetting critical tasks.

6. Balancing Workload and Avoiding Overcommitment

An excessive workload and constant overcommitment can lead to burnout and increased stress levels. Encouraging employees to assess their workload realistically and set boundaries on their time commitments can prevent overwhelming situations.

7. Flexibility and Adaptability in Time Management

While effective time management is essential, it's equally important to be flexible and adaptable. Unexpected situations or emergencies may arise, requiring adjustments to schedules and priorities. Promoting a supportive and understanding work environment can help employees manage unexpected challenges without undue stress.

In Summary

Effective time and task management play a vital role in reducing workplace stress, improving productivity, and fostering a healthier work-life balance. By prioritizing tasks, setting realistic goals, avoiding multitasking, and utilizing time management tools, individuals can enhance their performance and overall well-being. In combination with a resilient mindset, efficient time and task management contribute to a positive work culture that supports employee success and satisfaction. In the following chapters, we will explore additional stress management techniques that complement effective time management, providing a comprehensive approach to workplace well-being.

Chapter 5

Creating a Supportive Work Environment

Introduction:
In Chapter 4, we discussed effective time and task management as essential components of managing workplace stress. In this chapter, we will focus on the significance of creating a supportive work environment to complement these strategies. A supportive work environment promotes well-being, reduces stress, and enhances overall job satisfaction. It involves fostering positive workplace culture, encouraging open communication, and prioritizing work-life balance.

1. The Role of Workplace Culture in Stress Management

Workplace culture refers to the values, beliefs, and norms shared among employees and leadership. A positive and supportive workplace culture can significantly impact stress management. Creating a culture that prioritizes employee well-being and recognizes the importance of work-life balance can lead to a more resilient and engaged workforce.

2. Strategies for Fostering a Supportive and Positive Work Environment

- Employee Recognition and Appreciation: Recognizing employees' efforts and accomplishments boosts morale and fosters a sense of value within the organization.
- Transparent Communication: Encouraging open and transparent communication between management and employees creates a culture of trust and reduces uncertainties.
- Flexibility in Work Arrangements: Offering flexible work arrangements, such as remote work options or flexible hours, supports employees in managing their personal and professional responsibilities effectively.
- Employee Wellness Programs: Implementing wellness programs that address physical and mental health can contribute to a healthier workforce and reduce stress levels.

- Fair and Consistent Policies: Ensuring that workplace policies are fair, consistent, and supportive fosters a sense of security and reduces stress related to uncertainties or inequities.

3. Building Strong Relationships and Open Communication with Colleagues

Positive relationships with colleagues contribute to a supportive work environment. Encouraging teamwork, collaboration, and empathy among employees can create a sense of camaraderie and support during challenging times.

4. Encouraging Work-Life Balance

Work-life balance is a critical aspect of stress management. Encouraging employees to prioritize their well-being outside of work contributes to overall job satisfaction and reduces the risk of burnout. Strategies to encourage work-life balance include:

- Setting Boundaries: Encouraging employees to set clear boundaries between work and personal time.

- Offering Paid Time Off: Providing sufficient paid time off for vacations, personal days, and sick leave.

- Creating a Culture of Work-Life Balance: Promoting a culture where taking breaks and time off is encouraged rather than frowned upon.

5. Providing Stress Management Resources and Support

Offering stress management resources and support within the workplace can be invaluable. This may include workshops on stress reduction techniques, access to mental health resources, or counseling services.

6. Empowering Employees in Decision-making

Empowering employees to have a say in decisions that affect their work can contribute to a sense of control and autonomy. This can reduce feelings of stress related to a lack of control over one's work environment.

In Summary

Creating a supportive work environment is essential for effectively managing workplace stress and promoting overall well-being. By fostering a positive workplace culture, encouraging open communication, supporting work-life balance, and providing stress management resources, organizations can cultivate a more resilient and engaged workforce. In combination with effective time and task management and a resilient mindset, a supportive work environment enhances stress management efforts and contributes to a positive and thriving workplace. In the following chapters, we will explore additional stress management techniques that complement a supportive work environment, providing a comprehensive approach to employee well-being and job satisfaction.

Chapter 6

Stress-Relief Techniques at Work

Introduction:
In Chapter 5, we discussed the importance of creating a supportive work environment to manage workplace stress effectively. In this chapter, we will explore stress-relief techniques that can be implemented directly in the workplace. These techniques empower employees to take proactive steps to reduce stress during their workday, promoting a healthier and more positive work environment.

1. Quick and Simple Stress-Relief Exercises for the Workplace

- Deep Breathing Exercises: Practicing deep breathing techniques, such as diaphragmatic breathing or the 4-7-8 technique, can help calm the nervous system and reduce stress levels.

- Progressive Muscle Relaxation: Tensing and relaxing different muscle groups in the body can release physical tension and promote relaxation.
- Stretching: Simple stretches at the desk or in a designated area can alleviate muscle stiffness and improve circulation.
- Chair Yoga: Gentle chair yoga poses can be performed to relax the body and mind without leaving the workspace.
- Mindful Moments: Encouraging short mindful moments throughout the day, such as pausing to focus on the senses or taking a mindful walk, can provide moments of relaxation and rejuvenation.

2. Breathing Techniques, Mindfulness Practices, and Relaxation Exercises

- Breathing Techniques: Instructing employees in various breathing exercises can provide a quick and accessible tool for reducing stress on the spot.
- Mindful Meditation: Guided mindfulness meditation sessions can be offered during breaks to promote relaxation and mental clarity.
- Visualization: Encouraging employees to visualize calming and positive scenes can help shift focus away from stressors and induce relaxation.

- Body Scans: Leading employees through body scan exercises to become aware of tension and release it can reduce physical stress symptoms.

3. Incorporating Movement and Physical Activity into the Workday

- Active Breaks: Encouraging employees to take short breaks for physical activity, such as walking or stretching, can combat sedentary behavior and improve mood.
- Walking Meetings: Consider conducting walking meetings, especially for one-on-one discussions, to combine productivity with physical movement.
- Desk Exercises: Providing guidelines for discreet exercises that can be done at the desk, like desk push-ups or leg lifts, can promote circulation and energy.

4. Setting Up a Calming Workspace to Promote Well-Being

- Personalizing Workspace: Allowing employees to personalize their workspace with calming elements, such as plants, soothing colors, or personal photos, can create a more comforting environment.

- Noise Reduction: Implementing measures to reduce noise distractions, such as providing noise-canceling headphones or designated quiet areas, can enhance focus and reduce stress.

5. Promoting Work-Life Integration

- Flexible Breaks: Encouraging employees to take breaks when needed, even if it means stepping outside for fresh air, can contribute to work-life integration and stress reduction.
- Implementing a 'No After-Hours Email' Policy: Setting clear boundaries regarding responding to work-related emails after work hours can promote work-life balance and reduce stress.

6. Mindful Eating and Hydration

- Encouraging Mindful Eating: Raising awareness about mindful eating practices can help employees focus on their meals and enjoy them fully, reducing stress-related eating habits.
- Hydration Stations: Providing access to water stations or encouraging employees to keep water bottles at their desks can promote hydration, which plays a role in stress reduction.

In Summary

Incorporating stress-relief techniques directly into the workplace empowers employees to manage stress effectively throughout their workday. By providing quick and accessible methods for stress reduction, promoting a calming and supportive workspace, and encouraging work-life integration, organizations can foster a healthier and more positive work environment. These stress-relief techniques, in combination with a supportive workplace culture and resilience-building strategies, contribute to a comprehensive approach to stress management that benefits both employees and the organization as a whole. In the following chapters, we will explore additional stress management techniques to enhance workplace well-being and productivity.

Chapter 7

Coping with Difficult Situations and Difficult People

Introduction:

In Chapter 6, we discussed stress-relief techniques at work to help employees manage stress throughout their workday. In this chapter, we will focus on coping with difficult situations and difficult people, as these challenges can significantly impact workplace stress levels. Equipping employees with effective coping strategies can help reduce stress and improve interactions in challenging circumstances.

1. Identifying Difficult Situations in the Workplace

Difficult situations in the workplace can vary, but common examples include tight deadlines, conflicts with colleagues or supervisors, unexpected changes, and high-pressure projects. Identifying these situations early allows employees to be proactive in managing their stress response.

2. Strategies for Managing Difficult Situations

- Time Management and Prioritization: When faced with multiple demands and tight deadlines, employees can utilize effective time management techniques to prioritize tasks and stay focused on the most critical objectives.
- Communication and Collaboration: Encouraging open and honest communication among team members can help address issues promptly and collaboratively find solutions.
- Seeking Support: Encouraging employees to seek support from colleagues, mentors, or supervisors during difficult situations can provide valuable perspectives and guidance.
- Resilience and Problem-Solving: Drawing upon resilience-building skills, employees can approach challenges with a growth mindset, viewing them as opportunities for problem-solving and growth.

3. Understanding Difficult People and Managing Interactions

Difficult people in the workplace can create tension and stress for those around them. Understanding different personality types and conflict management styles can help employees navigate challenging interactions.

4. Conflict Resolution Techniques

- Active Listening: Encouraging active listening during conflicts can foster understanding and empathy, facilitating more constructive conversations.
- Assertiveness and Diplomacy: Teaching employees to assertively express their needs while maintaining diplomacy can prevent escalation of conflicts.
- Finding Common Ground: Identifying areas of agreement and common goals can help build bridges and create a more collaborative atmosphere.

5. Emotional Regulation and Stress Reduction during Difficult Interactions

- Stress-Awareness: Encouraging employees to be aware of their stress levels during difficult interactions can help them manage their emotions and responses effectively.

- Taking a Pause: Suggesting employees take a short break before responding to difficult situations can prevent impulsive reactions driven by stress.

- Practicing Empathy: Cultivating empathy toward difficult colleagues can help employees understand their perspectives and respond with greater understanding.

6. Strategies for Setting Boundaries

- Communicating Boundaries: Encouraging employees to communicate their boundaries assertively but respectfully can help prevent stress from overcommitment and allow for a healthier work-life balance.

- Saying No: Providing guidance on saying "no" when appropriate can help employees avoid overwhelming situations and maintain their well-being.

In Summary

Coping with difficult situations and difficult people is an essential aspect of managing workplace stress.

By equipping employees with effective coping strategies and conflict resolution techniques, organizations can foster a positive and supportive work environment. Encouraging open communication, resilience, and empathy can improve interactions and reduce stress in challenging circumstances. In combination with stress-relief techniques at work and a supportive workplace culture, coping with difficult situations becomes more manageable, contributing to a healthier and happier workforce. In the following chapters, we will explore additional stress management techniques that complement coping strategies, creating a comprehensive approach to workplace well-being and productivity.

Chapter 8

Nurturing Self-Care Outside of Work

Introduction:

In Chapter 7, we discussed coping with difficult situations and difficult people in the workplace to manage workplace stress effectively. In this chapter, we will focus on the importance of nurturing self-care outside of work as an essential aspect of stress management. Encouraging employees to prioritize self-care activities in their personal lives can significantly impact their overall well-being and resilience in handling workplace stress.

1. Understanding the Importance of Self-Care

Self-care involves taking intentional actions to promote physical, mental, and emotional well-being. It plays a crucial role in managing stress and preventing burnout. Encouraging employees to make time for self-care outside of work supports their ability to handle workplace challenges with greater ease and positivity.

2. Prioritizing Rest and Sleep

Restful sleep is essential for rejuvenating the body and mind. Encouraging employees to prioritize getting enough sleep by establishing a consistent sleep schedule and creating a calming bedtime routine can lead to better stress management and increased resilience.

3. Physical Activity and Exercise

Regular physical activity has numerous benefits for stress reduction and overall health. Encouraging employees to engage in regular exercise, whether it's a favorite sport, yoga, dancing, or simply going for a walk, can release endorphins and reduce stress levels.

4. Hobbies and Creative Outlets

Engaging in hobbies and creative outlets outside of work can provide a sense of fulfillment and relaxation. Encouraging employees to pursue activities they enjoy, such as painting, gardening, playing a musical instrument, or writing, can be a valuable stress-relief strategy.

5. Spending Quality Time with Loved Ones

Nurturing personal relationships and spending quality time with loved ones is vital for emotional well-being. Encouraging employees to make time for family and friends can strengthen social support systems, which play a significant role in managing stress.

6. Mindfulness and Meditation in Personal Life

Practicing mindfulness and meditation techniques outside of work can help employees manage stress and improve their overall resilience. Encouraging mindfulness practices during personal time can provide employees with a sense of balance and inner calm.

7. Digital Detox

In today's digital age, it's essential to take breaks from screens and technology. Encouraging employees to disconnect from their devices during personal time and engage in tech-free activities can contribute to better stress management and mental well-being.

8. Nutrition and Healthy Eating

Eating a balanced and nutritious diet is essential for overall health and well-being. Encouraging employees to make mindful food choices can support their physical and mental resilience.

9. Setting Boundaries between Work and Personal Life

Encouraging employees to set clear boundaries between work and personal life helps prevent work-related stress from spilling over into their personal time. Promoting the importance of unplugging from work emails and responsibilities during off-hours fosters work-life balance.

In Summary

Nurturing self-care outside of work is a critical component of effective stress management. By prioritizing rest and sleep, engaging in physical activity, pursuing hobbies, spending time with loved ones, and practicing mindfulness and meditation, employees can enhance their overall well-being and resilience. Encouraging employees to set boundaries between work and personal life further supports stress reduction and work-life integration. In combination with coping strategies, stress-relief techniques at work, and a supportive workplace culture, nurturing self-care outside of work creates a holistic approach to workplace well-being and productivity. In the final chapter, we will summarize the key points and reinforce the significance of a comprehensive approach to managing workplace stress.

Chapter 9

Addressing Burnout and its Consequences

Burnout has become a prevalent issue in today's fast-paced and demanding work environments. Excessive and protracted stress is the source of this state of emotional, mental, and bodily weariness. When employees experience burnout, their motivation, productivity, and overall well-being suffer significantly, leading to decreased job satisfaction and increased turnover rates. Addressing burnout and its consequences is crucial for maintaining a healthy and productive workforce.

1. Understanding Burnout and Its Causes

In this section, the book delves into a comprehensive explanation of burnout, exploring its various dimensions and manifestations. It discusses the physical and psychological symptoms associated with burnout, such as chronic fatigue, cynicism, and reduced professional efficacy. Readers gain insights into the emotional toll that burnout can take on individuals and how it can impact their relationships both inside and outside the workplace.

Furthermore, the book explores the common causes of burnout in the workplace. These causes often include excessive workload, lack of control over one's job, insufficient support from supervisors and colleagues, and a perceived lack of recognition for one's efforts. By understanding the root causes of burnout, organizations can begin to identify potential risk factors within their work environment and take proactive measures to prevent burnout among their employees.

2. Preventing and Combating Burnout in the Workplace

This section focuses on practical strategies and best practices that organizations can adopt to prevent and combat burnout effectively. It emphasizes the role of leadership in recognizing the signs of burnout and fostering a culture that prioritizes employee well-being.

One key approach discussed is the importance of work-life balance. The book explores how promoting a healthy work-life balance can reduce the risk of burnout by helping employees manage their stress levels and allocate time and energy to other important aspects of their lives. Strategies such as implementing flexible work hours, encouraging employees to take regular breaks, and offering paid time off are examined in detail.

Moreover, the book delves into the significance of employee recognition and appreciation. Recognizing employees for their efforts and contributions can boost morale and motivation, reducing the risk of burnout associated with feeling undervalued or unacknowledged. It provides practical tips for implementing recognition programs and initiatives that resonate with the organization's culture.

3. Supporting Employees Recovering from Burnout

When employees experience burnout, it is crucial for organizations to provide the necessary support and resources to facilitate their recovery. This section highlights the importance of open communication channels, allowing employees to voice their concerns without fear of judgment or reprisal. It suggests establishing confidential employee assistance programs that offer counseling services, stress management workshops, and other resources to help employees cope with burnout.

Additionally, the book explores the role of managers and colleagues in supporting individuals recovering from burnout. By fostering a compassionate and empathetic work environment, organizations can create a sense of belonging and promote a culture of support, encouraging individuals to seek help and take the necessary time off to recover fully.

Ultimately, this section aims to equip readers with the knowledge and tools needed to address burnout proactively and create a workplace that prioritizes employee well-being. By acknowledging and taking action to combat burnout, organizations can enhance employee engagement, retention, and overall productivity while cultivating a healthier and more sustainable work environment.

Chapter 10

Building a Culture of Wellbeing

In this critical section of the book, the focus is on cultivating a culture of wellbeing within the workplace. A culture of wellbeing encompasses the collective values, attitudes, and behaviors that prioritize and promote the physical, emotional, and mental health of employees. It goes beyond merely implementing isolated wellness programs and becomes an integral part of the organization's identity and daily operations.

1. The Role of Organizational Culture in Stress Management

The chapter begins by explaining the significant influence that organizational culture has on stress management and overall employee well-being. It explores how a positive and supportive culture can serve as a protective factor against workplace stress and burnout. By fostering an environment that values work-life balance, employee health, and open communication, organizations can significantly reduce stress levels and enhance employee resilience.

The book emphasizes that creating a culture of wellbeing requires a top-down approach, with leaders and managers serving as role models for healthy behaviors and stress management techniques. When leadership actively supports and prioritizes employee well-being, it sends a clear message to the entire organization about the importance of taking care of oneself and others.

2. Promoting Work-Life Integration from the Top Down

This section delves deeper into the concept of work-life integration, as opposed to mere work-life balance. It encourages organizations to recognize that employees have multifaceted lives and responsibilities beyond the workplace. Instead of trying to compartmentalize work and personal life, work-life integration encourages finding ways to harmonize the two spheres.

The book discusses how organizations can lead by example in promoting work-life integration. This may involve offering flexible work arrangements, such as remote work options or flexible hours, to allow employees to better manage their personal commitments while meeting their work responsibilities. It also explores the benefits of setting clear boundaries to prevent work from encroaching on personal time and vice versa.

3. Sustaining a Healthy Work Environment

In this section, the book emphasizes the importance of continuity and consistency in maintaining a healthy work environment. It highlights the need for ongoing efforts to reinforce the culture of wellbeing and stress management throughout the organization.

To achieve sustainability, the book explores various strategies, including:

- Regularly assessing employee needs and feedback: Organizations should conduct surveys and gather feedback to understand the evolving needs of their employees. This information can guide the development of targeted wellness initiatives and ensure that the organization remains responsive to the changing concerns of its workforce.

- Providing continuous education and training: Employee education on stress management, mindfulness, and other wellness practices should be an ongoing process. Regular workshops, webinars, and training sessions can reinforce the importance of employee wellbeing and equip employees with practical tools to manage stress effectively.

- Recognizing and celebrating successes: Organizations should acknowledge and celebrate the positive impact of their stress management efforts. Recognizing teams and individuals who contribute to a healthy work culture fosters a sense of achievement and motivation to continue those practices.

- Integrating wellness into company policies: To sustain a culture of wellbeing, organizations should integrate wellness considerations into their policies and procedures. For example, incorporating wellbeing goals into performance evaluations can reinforce the organization's commitment to employee health and happiness.

By implementing these strategies, organizations can create a workplace that not only effectively manages stress but actively promotes the overall health and wellbeing of its employees. A sustained culture of wellbeing not only benefits individual employees but also enhances organizational performance, productivity, and reputation in the long run.

Chapter 11

Case Studies: Successful Stress Management Strategies

This section of the book presents real-life case studies of organizations that have successfully implemented stress management strategies and created healthier work environments for their employees. Each case study provides valuable insights into the specific challenges faced by the organizations, the strategies they adopted, and the positive outcomes they achieved.

1. Company A: Creating a Supportive and Stress-Reducing Workplace

In this case study, Company A, a medium-sized technology firm, struggled with high turnover rates and declining employee morale. The chapter explores how the company's leadership recognized the impact of workplace stress on these issues and decided to take proactive measures to address the problem.

The book delves into the steps taken by Company A, which included:

- Conducting a comprehensive stress assessment: The organization started by conducting an anonymous stress survey to understand the specific stressors affecting its employees. This survey helped identify key stress points, such as excessive workloads and limited growth opportunities.

- Redesigning work processes: Based on the survey results, the company reevaluated its work processes and implemented changes to reduce unnecessary bureaucratic procedures and streamline workflows. This not only alleviated stress but also improved overall efficiency.

- Enhancing employee support systems: Company A introduced support mechanisms, such as regular one-on-one meetings between managers and employees, to provide a safe space for discussing concerns and seeking guidance. Additionally, the organization promoted the use of employee assistance programs and mental health resources to support employees' well-being.

- Promoting work-life balance: The company encouraged flexible work arrangements, allowing employees to adjust their schedules to accommodate personal commitments. They also instituted a "wellness day" policy, granting employees an extra day off every quarter to focus on self-care.

The chapter discusses how these measures contributed to a significant reduction in stress levels among employees, resulting in increased job satisfaction and a noticeable decline in turnover rates.

2. Company B: Implementing Employee Wellness Programs with Impact

Company B, a large financial institution, faced challenges related to employee burnout and absenteeism. In this case study, the book explores how the organization proactively invested in employee wellness programs to tackle these issues.

The book discusses the successful initiatives implemented by Company B:

- Wellness workshops and seminars: The organization conducted regular workshops on stress management, mindfulness, and resilience. These workshops equipped employees with practical tools to manage stress effectively and cope with demanding situations.

- Physical health programs: Recognizing the connection between physical and mental health, the company initiated fitness programs, healthy eating initiatives, and onsite health screenings. These programs not only improved employees' physical health but also positively impacted their mental well-being.

- Mental health awareness campaigns: To reduce the stigma surrounding mental health, Company B launched awareness campaigns and training sessions for employees and managers. The goal was to foster a culture where employees felt comfortable discussing mental health challenges and seeking support when needed.

- Flexible work options: Understanding that work-related stress could be exacerbated by long commutes and rigid schedules, the organization implemented flexible work arrangements and remote work options to accommodate employees' individual needs.

The book highlights how Company B's commitment to employee wellness contributed to a more engaged and motivated workforce, resulting in reduced burnout rates and improved overall organizational performance.

3. Company C: Addressing Burnout and Improving Employee Engagement

Company C, a mid-sized marketing agency, faced significant issues with employee burnout, leading to decreased productivity and creativity among its teams. This case study examines the organization's journey toward addressing burnout and fostering a more positive and engaging work culture.

The book explores the strategies employed by Company C, such as:

- Reducing workload and setting realistic expectations: The organization reevaluated project deadlines and workloads to ensure that employees were not overwhelmed. Managers worked closely with teams to set achievable goals and provide necessary resources.

- Encouraging creativity and autonomy: Company C introduced initiatives to encourage employee creativity and autonomy in their work. This included allowing employees to pursue personal projects and offering opportunities for skill development and cross-functional collaboration.

- Recognition and rewards: The organization implemented a peer-recognition program, allowing employees to acknowledge their colleagues' efforts and contributions. Additionally, they established performance-based rewards and incentives to recognize exceptional work.

- Mental health support: Company C partnered with mental health professionals to provide counseling and support services to employees struggling with burnout or other stress-related issues.

The chapter discusses how these interventions resulted in a significant reduction in burnout rates and an increase in employee engagement and job satisfaction. Furthermore, Company C saw a surge in creativity and innovation, leading to improved client satisfaction and business growth.

By presenting these diverse case studies, the book offers readers a range of practical examples and valuable lessons on how organizations can implement effective stress management strategies and create a culture that prioritizes employee well-being. Each case study highlights the importance of tailored approaches that consider the unique challenges and needs of individual organizations and their workforce.

Chapter 12

Looking Ahead: Trends in Workplace Stress Management

In this forward-looking section of the book, the focus shifts to emerging trends and innovations in workplace stress management. As workplaces continue to evolve, new challenges and opportunities arise, and it is essential for organizations to stay informed about the latest developments in stress management to ensure the well-being of their employees.

1. Technological Innovations and Their Impact on Stress

This chapter examines the influence of technology on workplace stress and explores innovative ways technology can be leveraged to manage and reduce stress levels. It delves into how modern tools, such as artificial intelligence and machine learning, can be utilized to analyze employee data and identify patterns related to stress and burnout. By analyzing this data, organizations can proactively address stress triggers and design targeted interventions.

Additionally, the book discusses the increasing popularity of stress management apps and platforms. These apps offer personalized stress-reduction techniques, mindfulness exercises, and resilience-building tools that employees can access at their convenience. Furthermore, the chapter examines the potential role of virtual reality (VR) technology in creating immersive relaxation experiences to help employees de-stress during or after work hours.

2. The Future of Work-Life Balance

As workforces become more diverse and global, the concept of work-life balance is evolving. This chapter explores how the traditional boundaries between work and personal life continue to blur and the implications this has on employee stress. It discusses the rise of remote work, freelancing, and gig economy jobs, and how these work arrangements impact stress levels.

Furthermore, the book examines innovative work-life integration practices that allow employees to achieve better harmony between their professional and personal responsibilities. Organizations are experimenting with results-oriented work environments, where employees are evaluated based on their output rather than hours worked. This approach empowers employees to manage their schedules more effectively and reduces stress associated with rigid work hours.

3. Resilience Training for Employees

Resilience training has gained traction as a preventive measure to combat workplace stress. This chapter delves into the concept of resilience and how organizations can implement training programs to equip employees with the skills needed to cope with stress and adversity effectively.

Resilience training typically includes cognitive-behavioral techniques, mindfulness practices, and emotional intelligence development. By providing employees with these tools, organizations can foster a workforce that can better handle stressors, bounce back from setbacks, and maintain a positive and productive mindset.

4. Diversity, Inclusion, and Stress Management

The book also explores the relationship between workplace diversity, inclusion, and stress management. A diverse and inclusive work environment fosters a sense of belonging and psychological safety, reducing the stress associated with feelings of isolation or discrimination.

The chapter discusses the importance of diverse leadership and representation and how organizations can create inclusive policies and practices that support employees from all backgrounds. It also examines the benefits of employee resource groups and allyship programs in promoting an inclusive and supportive workplace culture.

In Summary

This forward-looking section of the book provides readers with insights into the evolving landscape of workplace stress management. By understanding and embracing these emerging trends, organizations can proactively address stress-related issues and cultivate a work environment that promotes employee well-being, productivity, and overall satisfaction. As the workplace continues to change, staying informed about these trends will be vital for creating healthier and more resilient workforces in the future.

Conclusion

In the ever-evolving landscape of today's workplaces, stress management is a critical component for maintaining a healthy and thriving workforce. Throughout this comprehensive exploration of stress management strategies, we have emphasized the importance of nurturing self-care both within and outside of work. The journey to reducing workplace stress does not end when the office doors close; rather, it extends into the personal lives of employees, where self-care practices play a transformative role in promoting overall well-being and resilience.

By fostering a supportive work environment, encouraging stress-relief techniques at work, and equipping employees with coping strategies for difficult situations and interactions, organizations lay the foundation for a healthier work culture. However, it is equally crucial to acknowledge that the journey towards stress management and well-being continues outside the workplace.

Nurturing self-care is not a luxury; it is a necessity for maintaining a balanced and fulfilling life. Prioritizing restful sleep, engaging in physical activities, spending quality time with loved ones, pursuing hobbies, and practicing mindfulness are all vital components of self-care that empower individuals to rejuvenate and recharge their mental and emotional reserves.

Organizations that recognize the significance of self-care foster a culture that values employees as whole individuals, beyond their roles in the workplace. Encouraging employees to prioritize self-care sends a powerful message of support and understanding, fostering a positive work-life integration and reducing the risk of burnout.

As employees embrace self-care practices, they strengthen their resilience and enhance their ability to cope with workplace stress. By nurturing their well-being outside of work, individuals create a robust foundation that enables them to approach challenges with greater clarity, emotional balance, and adaptability.

In conclusion, a comprehensive stress management approach goes beyond the confines of the workplace and extends into the personal lives of employees. Nurturing self-care outside of work is a vital aspect of this approach, empowering individuals to maintain a healthier work-life balance, build resilience, and navigate stress with grace and positivity.

As we strive for professional success and fulfillment, let us not overlook the importance of self-care. By investing in our well-being, we not only improve our individual lives but also contribute to a more compassionate, supportive, and productive work environment. Let us embrace self-care as an essential tool for managing workplace stress, unlocking our full potential, and creating a more balanced, fulfilled, and harmonious life.

9 798853 579101